CENTENNIAL COMMEMORATIVE
ISSUE

1872 1972

This Book and its companion
pure silver Coin-medal are issued
to commemorate the 100th Anniversary
of the Osage Reservation

———————

*September 30, 1972*

And is limited to 15,000 copies
No. *16225*

*Sylvester J. Tinker*

*Photograph by John (*

THE WEALTH OF THE OSAGE is reflected not only in oil and agriculture but a
the beauty of their land and the pride of their people.

# THE

# OSAGE

# PEOPLE

*by W. David Baird, Ph. D.*

Scientific Editors: Henry F. Dobyns and Robert C. Euler
General Editor: John I. Griffin

PUBLISHED BY INDIAN TRIBAL SERIES / PHOENIX

Library of Congress Catalog Number 72-87871

PRINTED IN THE UNITED STATES OF AMERICA — Imperial Lithographers

ON THIS DAY, SEPTEMBER 30, 1972, the Osage People celebrate their Centennial Anniversary of their removal from Kansas to their new home in the Osage Nation. I wish to extend an invitation to the readers of this book to come and participate in this centennial celebration.

As Principal Chief of the Osage Tribe, it is my pleasure to personally extend my appreciation to Indian Tribal Series for including the Osage Tribe in their series of Indian Tribes.

By acquiring this book and coin-medal you will learn the history of the Great Osage Nation, the only Indian reservation in Oklahoma.

Funds received from this issue will assist the tribe to implement programs for the benefit of the Osage People.

Sylvester J. Tinker,
Principal Chief
Osage Tribe of Indians

# ABOUT THE PRINCIPAL CHIEF

SYLVESTER J. TINKER was born February 22, 1903, in Osage Indian Territory. His father was Frank Tinker, his mother Mary L. Revard Tinker. His parents chose their allotment of tribal land for themselves and their children near the present town of Skiatook, Oklahoma. Tinker himself attended grade school at Skiatook; afterwards he attended Kemper Military School at Boonville, Missouri, for four years.

In 1965 Tinker was appointed to the Governor's Interstate Indian Council; he served on the Council for six years. In 1966 he was elected to the Osage Tribal Council by members of the tribe for a four-year term. He was elected to a four-year term as Principal Chief of the Osage Nation in June, 1970.

During his years of service to the Osage Nation, Tinker has had a great interest in serving all Indian people as well as his own Osage. In his work he has learned many of the problems that confront the Indian. Because of this knowledge he has served them in such capacities as one of the first appointees to the newly-established Oklahoma Indian Affairs Commission.

For the past 45 years Tinker has lived on his farm near Pawhuska, where he farms and ranches on a small scale. He is married and has a daughter and three grand-children.

Sylvester J. Tinker

DURING THE 1920'S newspapers across the continent carried stories that brought the Osage Indians to the forefront of the American consciousness. Situated in what is now northeastern Oklahoma, their reservation had become a virtual fountain of black gold. Oil royalties paid to the tribe in 1920 alone provided the typical Indian family of an allotted husband, wife, and three children with an annual income in excess of $40,000. Pressured and harrassed by hundreds of hucksters, many Osages recklessly dissipated their enormous wealth. Tales circulated about how they built elaborate houses but spent nights in traditional tepees, and of purchasing costly automobiles though they were unable to drive. Such sensational accounts provided the only knowledge of the Osages that most Americans had. Unfortunately, they did not know that the tribe had a proud and ancient heritage, one as rich in tradition as any ethnic group.

According to Osage mythology, *Wa-kon-da,* the life force of the universe, sent the tribal ancestors from among the stars down to occupy the earth. In time and after much wandering, the People of the Sky met another people who were indigenous to the earth. The Land People and the Sky People soon amalgmated into one tribe, referring to themselves both as Children of the Middle Waters and, in their humility, Little Ones. At the dawn of Osage history, a council of Little Old Men — seers — organized every aspect of tribal life, contemplated the mysteries of the universe and rationalized the manifestations of *Wa-kon-da.*

Tribal legend asserts that the ancient Osages at one time lived east of the Mississippi River, first in the Piedmont region of Virginia and then in the Ohio Valley. French documents and recent archeological studies tend to confirm the course of these pre-historic wanderings, but more importantly they suggest that the Dhegiha Sioux, of which linguistic family the Osages were a part, attained a level of cultural expression never again matched north of the valley of Mexico. Later invasions and attacks by more eastern Indians, especially the Iroquoian people, brought an end to this elaborate and sophisticated culture and forced its participants to flee westward.

Matured as a people and society, the Children of the Middle Waters followed the Ohio River to its confluence with the Mississippi, turned up that mighty stream to its junction with the Missouri, then pushed to the upper reaches of the river that now bears their name. By 1673, the Osages were situated in what is now western Missouri with steep and forested hills to the south and east, grass-covered, undulating praries on the north, and infinite buffalo plains to the west. The emigration had been disconcerting, but the lushness of their new homeland demonstrated that *Wa-kon-da* had not deserted his people.

The new environment encouraged the ancient Osages to develop a culture somewhat dissimilar from that further eastward. They sustained themselves not only by hunting and gathering, but by agriculture as well. In fields averaging about one-third acre per person, the tribal women cultivated corn, squash, beans, pumpkin and potatoes, with corn the most significant. Pawpaws, haws, grapes, persimmons, hickory nuts, walnuts, hackberries, pecans and acorns gathered from the nearby forest supplemented the diet. Still more important was the meat furnished by deer, turkey, prairie chicken, skunk and buffalo.

To find, kill and process bison required the complete cooperation of the entire tribe. Each spring and autumn scouts located the herds on

3

the western plains, while simultaneously the principal chiefs selected the site of the hunting camp which soon was occupied by a majority of the tribe. At the proper moment, specially chosen hunters approached the herd from down wind, drove it carefully into a cordon of comrades who at a given moment stampeded the animals over a cliff. In the canyon bottom, other tribesmen killed the stunned or wounded animals and butchered them "on the skin," carefully preserving every portion of the carcass. Not only did the buffalo provide food, but it also furnished clothes, utensils, ornaments and even glue.

Dominated by the skin-covered tepee and temporary in nature, the buffalo hunting camps contrasted with the more permanent tribal settlements. On the Osage River, the Little Ones arranged their semi-permanent dwellings, at least for ceremonial purposes, in two groups representing the grand divisions of the tribe. The chiefs of each division resided opposite each other at a central location. The typical lodge followed either a circular or oblong ground plan and was constructed with hickory saplings stuck into the ground, tied at the top, interlaced with smaller saplings and covered with buffalo skins. An opening at top center provided exit for smoke, and one on the east served as a door. Though usually of modest size, these lodges could be 100 feet in length, 20 feet in width and 10 feet in height.

Though noted for their ability to walk or run great distances, the Little Ones relied for transportation first on the dog. These ever-present animals carried packs or pulled the familiar travois on the occasion of the semi-annual buffalo hunts. Horses, of course, displaced the dogs as the principal beasts of burden once they were secured in the early 18th Century from tribes to the south and west. The horse provided uncommon mobility for the Little Ones, but it was never as important to their culture as it was to that of the Cheyennes or Comanches. Still, when mounted, the Osage was an expert equestrian and a figure of beauty.

In personal appearance, the Little Ones had and their modern descendants have no peer. Washington Irving, a careful observer of the American aborigine, found them "the finest looking Indians. . .in the west." The men were tall, sometimes six and one-half feet, and perfectly proportioned. Their faces were dignified, their movements graceful, their chests expansive, waists narrow and limbs slender. They shaved their heads except for a two-or three-inch scalplock that extended from their foreheads to their necks. Clad in deerskin loin cloths, leggings and moccasins, Osage men painted and tatooed their bodies and wore earrings and bracelets. The women were considerably shorter than the men, stouter but as well built. They wore their hair long and flowing, tatooed their bodies more often than the men and adorned themselves with earrings and bracklets. Like the men, they fashioned their garments — dresses, leggings and moccasins — from deerskin.

The ancient Osages had an elaborate social and governmental structure. The tribe was organized into two grand divisions, the Sky People (*Tzi-Sho*) and the Land People (*Hunkah*). These grand divisions were then sub-divided into twenty-one smaller units, known as clans, each of which had a descriptive name from the animal kingdom or some cosmic phenomena. These various clans had ceremonial as well as actual prerogatives, especially on the occasion of buffalo hunts, war parties and child naming. Also, one clan within each grand division was responsible for the selection of the chief of each division. Chosen for life, the two chiefs had equal power, but the one selected by the Sky People served as the peace chief, while that chosen from among the Land People reigned as war chief. Though their authority was ultimate, the chiefs were by no means autocrats as they made all major decisions in light of the deliberations of the Little Old Men.

These governmental structures were of utmost importance, but the family fireplace provided

*Photograph by John Griffin*

RANDOLPH "SMOKY" LOOKOUT displays Osage traditional ceremonial dress and ornaments. Wide belt is fully beaded, bells add music to Osage dances.

the real foundation of Osage society. Men selected their wives from the grand division of which they were not a part. The marriage was motivated primarily by material considerations, with the bride being purchased from her father. The ceremony consisted only of a feast for the male relatives of the bride. Polygamy was practiced by the Osages; when a man married he had pre-emptory marriage rights to the sisters of his wife. Divorce was easy though a hard-working woman seldom found herself without a mate. A husband had a right to kill an unfaithful wife, yet adultery was not uncommon nor promiscuity infrequent. The children of the marriage union were reckoned to be of the father's division and clan, making Osage society patrilineal.

The Little Ones manifested a deep religious faith. Very early in pre-history, the Little Old Men concluded that *Wa-Kon-da* was the giver of all life, and that he lived within everything and every place, both celestial and terrestrial. Bodily life resulted and was sustained from the on-going clash of the forces of the earth with those of the sky. To be in tune with the life force, i.e. *Wa-kon-da*, was the objective of every Osage. Each morning, noon and evening supplications rose to him requesting a long and healthful life, protection in battle, and direction by day. Elaborate rituals developed that chronicled the

Osages' dependence upon *Wa-kon-da* which, once recorded, provided a literature unmatched in sensitivity and devotion.

Ceremony, oral tradition and symbolism were also very important in the life of the Children of the Middle Waters. There were special ceremonies for peace and for war and for the naming of children. An elaborate Rite of the Chiefs preserved an oral account of the organization of civil government at the dawn of tribal history. The hawk served as a symbol for the tribe, selected by the Little Old Men because of its courage, swiftness, silence and cleanliness. From the skin of this sacred bird the Osages made *waxobs,* or shrines, to depict the courage of the warriors of each group within the tribe. Tobacco also had special ceremonial significance: it was never smoked without prayers first being muttered to *Wa-kon-da.*

War was another integral part of the lifeways of the ancient Osages. Although basically a peaceful people, because of the need for revenge, honor or prize they sometimes found it propitious to engage in conflict with their neighbors. On such occasions the Little Old Men in their daily assembly smoked the ceremonial pipe of war, selected a leader for the war party and, after fasts, elaborate rituals and petitions to *Wa-kon-da,* sent him against the common enemy. Careful procedures were followed in the course of the mission, at the successful con-

10

clusion of which general rejoicing reigned among the Little Ones. Yet war for the Children of the Middle Waters was only a necessary evil, and though all men sought fame as a warrior, the highest honor was reserved for those excelling in the defense of lodge and field.

## THE OSAGES MEET THE WHITE MAN, 1673 TO 1803

By the mid-17th Century the sons of France, in quest of fur and access to the western sea, had pushed beyond their St. Lawrence River settlements to Lake Superior. There Indian accounts of a mighty river that drained the mid-section of the continent suggested the possibility of an inland passage to the Pacific and prospects of an immense empire of fur. Seeking to confirm the information, two of New France's more renowned explorers, Father Jacques Marquette and Louis Joliet, in June, 1673, descended the Wisconsin River to the fabled Father of Waters. Turning their canoes southward, they learned from natives at the mouth of the Arkansas River that the Mississippi coursed not to the Pacific but to the Gulf of Mexico where other Europeans, namely the Spaniards, already were living. Disappointed at not finding the western sea, the explorers nonetheless claimed the river valley for the King of France, declaring its inhabitants subjects of their sovereign, and turned back to Lake Michigan.

11

Most of the peoples whom Marquette and Joliet so easily placed in the orbit of France were unaware of the expedition. Yet the explorers knew of the existence of particular aboriginal groups because Illinois Indians in the course of the journey had identified them and their domains. The Illinois, for example, pointed to the region south and west of the mouth of the Missouri River as *Wah-Sha-She* country, an name Marquette Gallicized into *Ouazhagi* and the English later Anglicized to Osage. The *Wah-Sha-She*, of course, was only the most eastern clan of the Little Ones, but the distinction was lost on the Europeans.

Marquette's Indian guides also accurately located for him the principal villages of the Little Ones. The two largest settlements were situated on the south fork of the Osage River in what is now Vernon County, Missouri. The Little Osages occupied the most western site and the Great Osages the most eastern. Events in pre-history explained the physical division: once a great flood had forced residents of a single village to seek refuge, some on high ground and others at lower levels. Those who retreated to the heights became the Great Osages, and those who stayed at the lower level were the Little Osages. Unknown to Marquette, in 1673 the Little Ones also resided in smaller villages, one on the Marmiton River, another on the Missouri, and others elsewhere in the vicinity. Also, they

12

maintained semi-permanent hunting camps near the Three Forks region in eastern Oklahoma (where the Verdigris and the Neosho empty into the Arkansas) and on the Salt Fork of the Arkansas near modern Ponca City, Oklahoma. From these camps, the Osages wandered as far south as the Red River, as far north as the Platte and as far west as the Rocky Mountains.

Joliet and Marquette's exploration of the Mississippi valley and their identification of the natives stimulated a vital French expansion into the western waters. Where those two restless explorers had only heard of the various tribes, nameless *coureurs de bois* and *voyageurs* soon sought them out for purposes of commerce. To the villages of the Little Ones they brought guns, utensils, metal tools and alcoholic beverages. Awed by and envious of these manufactured goods, the Indians eagerly offered to exchange for them the products of their own culture and lifeways — furs the French could market in Europe and slaves they could sell in the Caribbean.

Though a mutually satisfying commerce ensued, the need to provide raw materials of the trade altered traditional behavioral patterns of the Little Ones. Where once they warred only for revenge or glory, now, on horses recently obtained and with flintlocks newly purchased, they launched attack after attack upon their traditional enemies in order to seize captives for the slave trade. Unarmed and ill mounted, the Pawnees, the Padoucas and the Caddoes proved no match for the Osage warriors. Also, where once the Little Ones hunted only for meat or raiment, now they sought beaver and deer for commercial purposes.

The French viewed the Osages as more than mere commercial partners. Living on a tributary of the Missouri River, the tribe, if so disposed, could prohibit any exploration of or traffic on that vital waterway. Anxious to exploit the potential of the river, the French sought the good will of the Little Ones with gifts, special consideration and diplomatic deference. The tribute not only won the confidence of the tribe, but it convinced the Osages of their own importance and detracted from their tendency toward humility.

By 1712 the Osage-French alliance had so developed that the Little Ones represented the best hope of France both west and east of the Mississippi River. For example, when the Fox Indians placed Fort Detroit under siege, Osage and Missouri Indian warriors rushed to the relief of that outpost, forcing the Fox to retreat in disarray. Etienne Venyard Bourgmont, one of the grateful French officers at Detroit, was so impressed by the Children of the Middle Waters that he deserted his command and returned with them to their homes. Especially infatuated with

14

a beautiful Missouri girl, he resided with her in her village, and fathered one child; he also explored the western waters, perhaps even journeying up the Platte to eastern Wyoming. Of towering physique, ferocious strength and eubulent personality, Bourgmont gained the affection and respect of the Little Ones and further committed the tribe to the French alliance.

Still, the initial European occupation of the lower Mississippi Valley had relatively little impact upon the Osages. All that changed when John Law's Company of the Indies assumed control of Louisiana in January, 1718. Authorities of the company believed that the Indian slave traffic along the Missouri so promoted inter-tribal turmoil that neither a profitable trade nor a systematic mineral exploitation was possible. Peaceful relations on the Missouri seemed to them absolutely essential. To that end, in 1719 the company sent Charles Claude du Tisne to the permanent villages of the Little Ones. Du Tisne explained to the tribe that the French expected to continue a beneficial trade with it, but he insisted that the disruptive traffic in slaves must cease. Furthermore, he informed the Osages, the French anticipated establishing regular commercial relations with the more western Indians, especially the Pawnee. That the traditional Indian enemy of the tribe should

AN OSAGE WEDDING PROCESSION. In the two days of preparation for an O
wedding, the groom sends food each day to his intended, to let her know what
of fare to expect after marriage. On the wedding day the bride dresses in all her
clothes and rides to the groom's house on a pony or in a carriage; a pony i
beside her. While she is on her way, other squaws race each other to her from
groom's house; the led pony goes to the first-place winner, and the second-

ners get the bride's fine clothes, ribbons and jewelry, leaving her with only one
e. At the groom's house she is lifted off the pony or carriage and carried inside
a blanket. The groom is called out of hiding and the two eat and drink together –
hey are happy about their parents' choice. The groom's parents support the
ple during their first year of marriage.

have French guns greatly disconcerted the Little Ones, yet for the moment they permitted the Frenchman to continue on to the Pawnees.

Obviously of economic significance, the mission of du Tisne had important strategic implications. Hopefully commerce with those Indians west of the Osages would pull them within the French orbit and provide a buffer against any Spanish expansion across the Plains into the Mississippi Valley. Further, the good will of the semi-nomadic tribes should permit a French trade with Spain's Rio Grande settlements if that trade ever became desirable. The strategy, however, did not take the Osages into account, a mistake made apparent during Bernard de la Harpe's first expedition up Red River in 1719. At a point near the Kiamichi Mountains his party of largely Caddo Indians almost disintegrated when it encountered by mere chance a group of giant-like Osage braves. The reaction suggested that the Little Ones undoubtedly could prevent the implementation of any French scheme not to their liking. In other words, to get *to* the southern Plains Indians the French must first get *through* the Osages.

To institute the policy the King of France sent back to Louisiana Etienne Bourgmont, who had returned to Paris to receive a decoration for his North America explorations. Promised reward and royal rank, Bourgmont was directed first to construct a fort on the Missouri River in order to check the Osage, and then to make treaties of alliance with the western tribes. Returning through New Orleans, the "Commandant of the Missouri" had constructed Fort Orleans by the summer of 1723. One-half of his mission completed, in July of the following year he ventured west with 100 Missouri and 64 Osage warriors to the Kansas Indian settlements to negotiate an inter-tribal peace and commercial accord. Though the Little Ones accompanied the commandant, they had little enthusiasm for his overture to the western tribes and soon abandoned the expedition to participate in the autumn buffalo hunt. The Frenchman, though, successfully established cordial relations with the Kansas and other Plains tribes.

To weld his alliances further, Bourgmont proposed that representatives of the different tribes, including the Osages, accompany him on a trip to France. The Plains Indians refused, but four Osages, five Missouri and four Illinois agreed to the proposal. After a long voyage across the Atlantic, the delegates from the western waters arrived in Paris on September 28, 1725. The visitors favorably impressed the royal entourage, and doubtlessly the American natives were equally awed by the refinements of European society. Whether the Osages returned to their villages is not recorded, but it is apparent that the overseas adventure and the sojourn of Bourgmont on the Missouri further enhanced the prestige of the French.

Yet the allegiance of the Osages had its limits, a fact that became apparent after 1739 when the Mallet brothers successfully crossed the prairies to the Rio Grande in order to trade with the Spaniards at Santa Fe. Such a commerce bypassed the Little Ones and eroded their position among the western tribes. Accordingly, when Fabry de la Bruyere in 1742 attempted to follow the Mallets to New Mexico, elements of the tribe intercepted the French party on the Canadian River, harrassed it and forced its retreat.

The Osages were just as inhospitable to the independent traders. They regularly attacked, dispossessed and sometimes killed those *coureurs de bois* who had the impudence to engage in commerce on the Red, Arkansas and the Missouri Rivers. French authority railed against them, but tribal good will was so necessary to France's ambition in North America that the depredations were generally overlooked.

The importance of the Osages to France became especially evident in the mid-18th Century. By then the greatest challenge to French interests came, not from Spain in New Mexico, but from England whose citizens disseminated superior trade goods west on the Ohio River and south from Hudson's Bay. To thwart the western expansion of England, the French relied primarily upon Indian allies. They expected the Little Ones, for example, to counter the British supplied Fox who occupied the area north of the Missouri. Additionally, the French looked to the Osages to assist in the defense of their possessions in the Ohio Valley. In 1755 they recruited and dispatched tribal warriors to Fort Duquesne in an attempt to repel a British challenge led by Gen. Edward Braddock. In July, the French Indians defeated the English column, killed its commander and forced its retreat.

But the victorious effort at the Forks of the Ohio did not save North America for France. A larger British colonial population and an immense advantage on the sea spelled the ultimate defeat of France, a defeat that was admitted at the Treaty of Paris in 1763. By terms of this settlement, the French ceded all of their possessions east of the Mississippi River to England and, as compensation for losses suffered elsewhere, presented to her ally, Spain, that area claimed west of the Mississippi. For the Osages, the treaty meant that in Louisiana Spanish authority would be substituted for that of France.

The implications of the Treaty of Paris were not immediately apparent to the Little Ones. The Europeans coming among them continued to be of French extraction; for that matter there were more French traders than ever before. Rather than suffer English rule, many who had lived in the Illinois country crossed the Mississippi and took up residence on its western bank in the older community of Ste. Genevieve or in the new settlement of St. Louis.

Still, the Spaniards were the sovereigns of the Missouri River country. And where the French had placated, over-looked or even spoiled the Osages, the new Louisiana authorities insisted that the Little Ones conform to established policy. They expected the tribe to cease the raids on traditional enemies that kept the region north of the Red River in constant turmoil. Accordingly, in 1777 the Spanish adopted a proposal of Anathase de Mezieres, commandant of the fort at Natchitoches, that he enlist 1270 warriors from the 10 tribes in his jurisdiction and march north to chastize the Osages. Though de Mezieres' war plan was never implemented, the goal of checking the Little Ones remained. Somewhat later, the Spaniards demanded that those tribal leaders residing at the hunting camp in the Three Forks region deliver certain chiefs to New Orleans. Held as hostages, these chiefs would presumably insure the good behavior of the tribal raiders. Members of the tribe did go to New Orleans, but the Osages continued to terrorize the southwest.

Unable to intimidate the Little Ones, the

Spaniards decided upon a policy of economic coercion. As early as 1790 they attempted to prevent St. Louis traders from engaging in commerce with the tribe. More and more dependent upon European manufactured items, the Osages, it was reasoned, would be brought to terms by a prohibition of trade. Six thousand in number, proud and convinced of their own importance, the Little Ones reacted to the new policy with characteristic vigor. Traders who sought to by-pass their villages were stopped, harrassed and relieved of their goods. Also, the grand peace chief sent a delegation of four sub-chieftains and thirty-two warriors to St. Louis to protest the policy.

But the Spanish would not be moved from their chosen course. In December, 1972 Hector Baron de Carondelet, the governor of New Orleans, reconfirmed the no-trade policy and, in the following June, took the ultimate step and declared war upon the Osages. Given Spain's military position in Louisiana, the declaration was foolhardy: it simply stirred the Little Ones to attack first. Ignoring St. Louis, tribal war parties hit Ste. Genevieve in January, 1794, killing one resident; elsewhere they scalped and murdered isolated traders. Since the Spaniards had not been prepared for such a reaction, de Carondelet promptly abandoned the war. Besides, with the expansion-minded United

States now in control of the eastern bank of the Mississippi, Spain needed the friendship of the Little Ones rather than their enmity.

At the moment of this realization, Auguste Chouteau arrived in New Orleans to make a momenteous request of Governor de Carondelet. As a boy of 15, Chouteau had assisted in the founding of St. Louis and had since conducted successful trading ventures among the Osages. Immensely respected by the Little Ones, the Frenchman asked de Carondelet for a six-year monopoly on all commerce with the tribe. In return for such a grant, Chouteau promised to establish a fort that would serve as a focus of Spanish authority throughout the region and provide a check on Osage depredations. With his former policy of threats and force so ineffective, the governor responded positively, almost gratefully, to the request.

By mid-summer 1795, Chouteau had established himself near the Great Osage village. The Little Ones watched with favor and fascination the construction of the fort the young Frenchman completed in August and christened "Fort Carondelet." For the next several years the commercial relations initiated by Chouteau proved beneficial for all parties. For the trader it brought prosperity, for the Indians a constant source of trade goods, and for Spain a faithful ally against foreign encroachment. The Little

24

Ones, however, did not cease their warlike habits and frequent depredations against isolated traders and Indian enemies. But Chouteau confined their raids to the upper Arkansas Valley and rationalized them as a small price to pay for Osage good will.

The situation instituted by Chouteau proved so satisfactory to Spain that in 1800 New Orleans officials extended his monopoly for four more years. Yet the Frenchman had reaped such a financial harvest that other traders soon coveted his exclusive rights. The most vigorous challenge came from Manuel Lisa, a Spaniard, who used the fact of his Latin birth to advance his own cause among Spanish authorities. Arguing that Chouteau had failed to promote agriculture and that only through farming could Spain really hold Louisiana, Lisa gained in June, 1802 the cancellation of Chouteau's monopoly and its transference to him.

Chouteau, however, was not to be out-maneuvered. Working with his half-brother and associate, Pierre, he persuaded Chief Cashesegra and at least one-half of the Great Osage village to take up permanent homes at the site of his Three Forks trading house. Though Cashesegra, with Chouteau's influence, a hereditary chieftain named Clermont, nominal leader of the "Arkansas Osage," became the most influential personality. Striking in appearance and capable in leadership, he left the Osage River settlements after his rights as chief had been usurped by Pawhuska, or "White Hair."

Upon removal to what is now eastern Oklahoma, the Arkansas Osages occupied a good country with excellent commercial possibilities. Draining a fine hunting region, the Three Forks was situated at the head of the navigation of the Arkansas River, where furs could be shipped to New Orleans and supplies could be received on return voyages. Chouteau had chosen well, so well that after 1802 the Three Forks region rather than the Osage River became the focus of tribal activity.

Throughout the period of European contact, the Osages had altered traditional habits and tastes as well as settlement location. A casual glance would suggest that the alterations were profound: they used guns instead of bows and arrows, rode horses rather than walked, used metal utensils rather than ones of stone and bone. Actually, these adaptations only facilitated traditional lifeways. Had the Osages lost access to the European refinements, they could have resumed their traditional habits with little difficulty. For that matter they consciously rejected institutions that might have seriously altered their culture patterns. They had not, for example, accepted the white man's God. Black robes — Jesuits priests — had worked among the Osages for more than a century without visible results. Still, the presence of the Europeans brought profound and lasting change in at least one area. The white man's demand for furs and need for meat had diminished the abundance of game throughout the Mississippi Valley and had pushed the buffalo ever farther westward. The loss was irreplaceable and the ecological imbalance permanent. The condition was fraught with implications for the future of the Little Ones.

## THE AMERICANS ARRIVE, 1803 TO 1839

By the turn of the century Spain had concluded that Louisiana was little more than a burden upon the imperial treasury. When Napoleon proposed that France reassume control of the province, the Spanish crown relinquished Louisiana in 1801 at the Treaty of San Ildefonso. News of the transfer panicked the United States government, since a powerful France might well block any future westward expansion of the young Republic. President Thomas Jefferson immediately directed American representatives in Paris to seek an accommodation with the Emperor. Having suffered serious reverses in his colonial schemes, Napoleon surprised the American officials and offered to sell all of Louisiana. Agreeing on a purchase price of $15 million, in 1803 the United States gained title to this broad expanse west of the Mississippi.

The following year President Jefferson sent out two expeditions — Lewis and Clark up the Missouri River and Hunter and Dunbar up the Red — to determine the extent, character and occupants of the country recently acquired. These and later parties, like the French and Spaniards before them, concluded that the Osages held the key to successful American control of Louisiana. To gain the friendship of the Little Ones, within the next four years the United States appointed the popular Pierre Chouteau as government agent, sent a delegation of impressionable chiefs to Washington, and directed the return of some 46 Osages held captive by the Potawatomi. It also established a trading factory at Fort Osage on the Missouri River near what is now Sibley, Missouri. As the "factory" provided quality goods at cost, it presumably would favorably dispose the Little Ones to the Americans and make them dependable allies and responsive to the goals of the federal government.

From the beginning, President Jefferson had conceived of Louisiana as an area where eastern Indians reluctant to adopt the white man's way might migrate. Once situated west of the Mississippi River, the emigrants might continue their aboriginal lifeways without obstructing the white man's exploitation of their ancestral domains. But such as objective did not take into account those tribes who already occupied

28

Louisiana. The Osages, for one, had no intention of permitting eastern tribes to encroach upon its hunting grounds. If any ever ventured across the Mississippi into what is now northern Arkansas or southern Missouri, they could expect attack, forfeiture of property and loss of life. Osage opposition undoubtedly endangered a successful removal program.

To facilitate its policy, the United States in November, 1808, summoned the Great and Little Osages to a council on the Missouri River. Meriwether Lewis and William Clark served as commissioners for the government, while White Hair acted as principal spokesman for the tribe. Influenced by Pierre Chouteau and threatened with a loss of trade goods, the Osages agreed to cede to the United States all of the country lying north of the Arkansas River and east of a north-south line that intersected the council grounds. As compensation, the United States promised the tribe a blacksmith, tools to mend guns, agricultural implements, an annuity of $1500, and payment of $5000 toward claims against it by white men.

Ratified by the Arkansas Osages the following year, the treaty quieted the claim of the Little Ones to substantially all of northern Arkansas and much of what is now the state of Missouri. The 52,000,000-acre region would presumably provide a resettlement area for eastern Indians. Indeed, in 1809 large numbers of Cherokees succumbed to government pressure and emigrated to the Arkansas River valley. The Cherokee agent, Maj. William L. Lovely, soon learned that the Osage cession did not mean that the Little Ones would welcome the emigrants. Despite his efforts at diplomacy throughout 1813, hostilities between Clermont's people and the Cherokee intruders frequently occurred.

That special attention must be paid the Little Ones became particularly apparent with the outbreak of war in 1812. When the American government simultaneously abandoned Fort Osage and rejected a tribal offer to aid in the struggle, some of the warriors journeyed to Prairie de Chien to receive presents from the English. The British even sent their flag to fly over the Osage villages. Realizing this mistake in ignoring the Little Ones, American commissioners in September, 1815 met representatives of the tribe near the mouth of the Missouri River to reestablish the *status quo ante-bellum.*

Nevertheless, the respect tendered the Osages did not last long. The Arkansas Osages continued to obstruct any meaningful removal policy by harrassing emigrant Cherokees who hunted their domain. In an attempt to settle the conflict, in June, 1816 Maj. Lovely persuaded Clermont's band to relinquish claims to land lying between the Verdigris River and the Arkansas Cherokee settlements. Known as

30

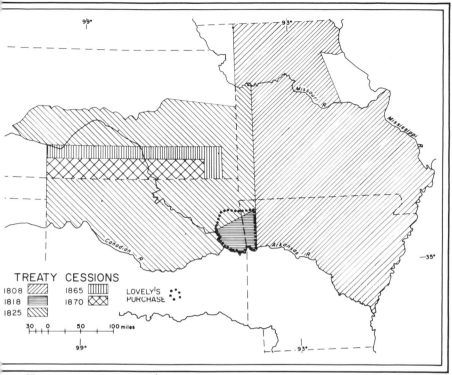

P 1. Treaty Cessions, 1808 thru 1870.

31

"Lovely's Purchase," this tract hopefully would provide a buffer between the tribes and leave the Cherokees free to hunt in peace. The agent's efforts were in vain, and hostilities continued unabated.

To redress the harrassment, the Cherokees and other emigrant Indians met in early 1817 to plan a combined attack upon Clermont's village. An invitation to join the war was sent to the eastern Cherokees still resident in the southern Appalachians. A number accepted the offer, one of whom, John McLamore, actually led the combined force of Cherokees, Choctaws, Chickasaws, Pawnees and Peorias that attacked the Verdigris settlement. Timing the assault to coincide with the autumn hunt when the men would be absent, the invaders succeeded in killing 83 women, children and old men and capturing 103 young girls and boys who could be sold as slaves. They set fire to the village and to the fields, then returned to their Arkansas River encampments with "glory and honor."

Though not entirely unhappy with the Battle of Claremore Mound, the United States realized Osage retaliation would be swift and general. As such a response would further impede Cherokee emigration, positive action was required immediately. Accordingly, in July, 1817, the Secretary of War ordered the establishment of a military post where the eastern Osage boundary intersected the Arkansas River. In December,

Maj. William Bradford began the construction of Fort Smith.

With the erection of Fort Smith, a Cherokee delegation simultaneously pressed upon Secretary of War John C. Calhoun the significance of their "victory" at Claremore Mound. Since the spoils of war always belonged to the victor, they argued, the government should assign a considerable portion of the Osage domain to their people. Calhoun accepted their view and ordered William Clark to compel the Osages to yield another slice of their land.

In September, 1818, Clark laid his instructions before the Great and Little Osages gathered at St. Louis and demanded that the tribe cede — this time legally — the "Lovely Purchase." The United States would compensate the tribe by paying claims against it in the amount of $4000. Also, the government would not transfer the "Purchase" to the Cherokees but hold it in trust for them as a hunting ground and western outlet. Signing the treaty as written, the Osages even entered into an agreement the next month with the Cherokees, pledging friendship and cessation of hostilities. On their part the emigrants agreed to return to Fort Smith the following spring those captives taken at the battle of Claremore Mound.

By virtue of the treaties and the construction of Fort Smith, the United States hoped that eastern Indian emigration would proceed and the turmoil on the Arkansas frontier cease. Yet any meaningful peace depended upon the acquiescence of the Arkansas Osage in the provisions of the two St. Louis agreements and the proper exchange of prisoners. Attaining those requisites proved difficult. Indeed, following the Cherokee attack upon his village, Clermont had called a general conference of Shawnee, Delaware, Creek, Quapaw, Kansas and Fox Indians. Presenting them with 300 horses, the chief sought to enlist them in some retaliatory action. But Maj. Bradford rushed to Clermont's town and quieted the Little Ones by assuring them that those Osages held prisoner by the Cherokee would be returned the following summer at Fort Smith.

Delighted with the prospect of seeing their women and children, Clermont and other Arkansas Osage chiefs journeyed to the fort in late July, 1819. The Cherokees failed to appear, explaining that they had to attend to their harvest. They did promise to return the captives in September. When that appointed day arrived the Cherokees were still absent, at which time Bradford ordered them to produce the prisoners. After further delays, the emigrants finally straggled in but even then with only a few of the captives. The bad faith of the Cherokees did not assuage the ill will of the Little Ones nor increase prospects for a successful policy of eastern Indian removal.

Though the emigrants had not fulfilled their part of the St. Louis bargain, they demanded that the Osages meet their pledges. The intruders were incensed when in February, 1820, a war band led by Mad Buffalo, Clermont's son, intercepted a Cherokee hunting party on Osage territory, killed three and took its store of furs. Nonetheless, Gov. James Miller of Arkansas Territory ignored emigrant demands for immediate retribution, noting that the Cherokees had failed to return all of the captives taken at the Battle of Claremore Mound. Rebuffed, they dropped plans for a combined tribal attack upon the Little Ones and delivered the prisoners that fall.

Gov. Miller hoped that conference and compromise would adjust the differences between the Osages and the Cherokees, but he misjudged both parties. For the Arkansas Osages the continued presence of the emigrants meant the rapid destruction of the game upon which their very lives depended. With their traditional livelihood in the balance, no real accommodation with the emigrants was possible. Neither did the Cherokees desire peace. In March, 1821 they informed Maj. Bradford that they would soon attack the Osages, justifying their aggression as necessary to secure richer lands for their growing agricultural economy.

The Little Ones struck first. In April, another war party led by Mad Buffalo descended the

Arkansas River to Fort Smith. Denied permission to enter the post, the Osages made 40 to 50 rafts in anticipation of crossing the river to the foot of the fort. When confronted with a six-pound cannon, they took their frustrations out on a Quapaw hunting party, killing and mutilating three of its members. Later, they murdered three Delaware Indians.

Mad Buffalo's raid produced consternation among both whites and Cherokees. The acting Governor of Arkansas Territory, Robert Crittenden, requested from the Secretary of War arms to "repel invasion and outrage," while the Cherokees gathered to defend their homes. The preparation was an unnecessary as it was hysterical. Clermont disavowed the action of his son and proposed a three-month armistice to be concluded by a permanent peace.

But the Cherokees wanted war, and Mad Buffalo's foray provided the pretext. They rejected Clermont's proposal and throughout the summer of 1821 planned a major attack upon the Little Ones. Maj. Bradford attempted to dissuade them and even promised to restrain any war party that sought to pass Fort Smith. Learning of Bradford's actions and assuming that he could control the emigrants, Clermont took his people to the Plains for their autumn hunt. This was precisely what the Cherokees wanted.

In October, 1821, more than 200 allied,

emigrant Indians headed up the Arkansas for the Verdigris. True to his word, Bradford intercepted the party; when the allies refused to turn back for some unexplained reason he furnished them with a barrel of gunpowder to use on the expedition. Proceeding to the nearly empty Osage villages, the invaders followed the trail of the Little Ones to the buffalo Plains. The allies attacked first the tribal camp, killing women, children and old men and taking some 30 captives. Their later assault on the able-bodied men did not fare so well; the Osages forced the Cherokees to retreat in disarray. Though hardly victorious, the invaders did disturb the autumn hunt and made the winter of 1821-22 a time of hunger for Clermont's people.

Though isolated retaliations for the attack occurred, the Osages were generally disposed to some kind of accommodation with the Cherokees. War weariness and 250 more troops stationed at Fort Smith enabled Nathanial Philbrook, the Osage subagent, to secure an armistice on May 16, 1822, and a promise from all parties to assemble in a peace conference the following June. On the appointed day, Clermont and 150 Osages met an equally large contingent of emigrant Cherokees at Fort Smith. On August 9, both groups accepted a written treaty, the principal feature of which was the return of 17 Osage prisoners held by the Cherokees, eight of whom were delivered on the spot with the remainder promised the following month. For the moment peace reigned on the Arkansas frontier.

As Clermont's band concluded its treaty with the Cherokees, those Osages still resident in Missouri signed yet another treaty with the United States on August 31, 1822. The provisions of the new agreement were simple: for merchandise valued at more than $2300 the Little Ones agreed to the abolition of the factory guaranteed them in the Treaty of 1808. Simple in meaning, the agreement had profound implications. With a government trading post no longer available, the Osages turned completely to private traders to obtain the items they so much desired. So the Chouteaus were soon able to induce them to leave their ancient villages and move southwest to the Neosho River near modern Salina, Oklahoma, where the Chouteau family had its center of operations. With the move to the Three Forks region, the Little Ones, 4500 strong, were again united.

A. P. Chouteau's commercial interests, of course, had been responsible for the initial division of the tribe; those same interests now reunited it. Whatever their internal situation the Little Ones had always served Chouteau well. Prior to 1812, tribal hunters annually exchanged at his Three Forks establishment $30,000 worth of beaver, otter, bear and bison skins for merchandise costing the Frenchman only $7500.

After 1817 they traded peltry valued at $80,000 to $100,000 for manufactured items costing less than one-half of that amount. No wonder the Chouteau family reigned supreme in St. Louis! Other renowned but less successful Three Forks traders included Nathaniel Pryor, Hugh Glenn and Sam Houston.

The settlement of even more Osages just west of the emigrant Cherokees was not calculated to perpetuate peace on the frontier nor was the increasing white population that drifted into the Indian country. Wholly unappreciative of the cultural and economic lifeways of the Indians, the American frontiersman refused to honor any boundary that might infringe upon his economic freedom. The Osages responded to the white intruder as they had to the earlier red emigrant. On November 17, 1823, for example, Mad Buffalo and 200 warriors intercepted a hunting party of white men and mixed-blook Quapaw Indians near Blue River, attacked it and left five men with their heads cut off and bodies mutilated. Col. Matthew Arbuckle, the new commander at Fort Smith, demanded that Clermont surrender the guilty warriors, a request the chief, as usual, graciously ignored.

To prevent similar Osage depredations the U.S. War Department ordered Arbuckle to remove the Fort Smith garrison to a point further west near the falls of the Verdigris. Established at Fort Gibson by mid-April 1824, the commander then renewed his demand that Clermont surrender Mad Buffalo. With the military only a few miles away, the chief had no practical alternative but to deliver his son and four others to Arbuckle that June. The Superior Court of the United States at Little Rock, after releasing three of the Osages, sentenced Mad Buffalo and Little Eagle to be hanged on December 21. Because of the deportment of the condemned, however, and because equally heinous Cherokee crimes had gone unpunished, President John Quincy Adams pardoned the two Osages and returned them to their people.

In the meantime, from his vantage point on the Verdigris, Col. Arbuckle instituted a plan he hoped would restrain the Little Ones. He believed a centralized tribal government led by a properly flattered Clermont could be induced to support United States Indian policy. Accordingly, he named a 13 member national council that duly elected Clermont as president. Directing the council to legislate on all important matters, he also established a national guard of 40 warriors to implement law and order. Though soon forgotten by the Little Ones, Arbuckle's plan foreshadowed a system of government successfully inaugurated in the late 19th Century.

The United States needed more from the Osages than just peaceful and democratic dispositions; the federal government needed their

40

land. In addition to the Cherokees, the government had re-settled smaller tribes — the Delaware, Kickapoo, Shawnee, Miami, Piankanshaw and Wea — in present southern Missouri and northern Arkansas. To preserve the tribes in the face of an ever-increasing white emigration into that region, federal authorities determined to send them even further west to lands then dominated by the Osages.

The United States directed William Clark to secure the desired re-settlement area from the Little Ones. Accordingly, on June 2, 1825 at St. Louis, Clark wrested from the Osages a relinquishment of any tribal claim to all lands west of Missouri and Arkansas Territory. Within the area ceded, however, the tribe reserved for its own settlement a tract 50 miles in width, originating 25 miles west of Missouri and extending to a line due south from the headwaters of the Kansas River. Altogether the tribe quitclaimed 45,000,000 acres of land. As compensation, the Little Ones were to receive merchandise valued at $7000 every year for 20 years, a number of domestic animals, forgiveness of debts at trading houses, payment of no more than $5000 in claims against them by American citizens, and an immediate gift of merchandise valued at $8600. The United States rationalized the Treaty of 1825 as necessary to "protect" the Osages from white emigrants, but William Clark, an honorable man, knew better: it was sheer extortion — an imposition of the strong upon the weak.

As was anticipated, immediately after the treaty White Hair the younger (the elder died in 1808) removed his people from the Grand Saline to the new Kansas reservation. Settling on the upper Neosho River, he was soon joined by the Little Osages, bringing the total population of the reserve to 3000. On the other hand, Clermont's band, long independent of the larger body, refused to move from the Three Forks region. Furthermore, it continued to resist red and white incursions into the traditional tribal domain despite the recent treaty.

The ability of the Arkansas Osages to resist was directly proportional to the number of emigrants resident among them. That number increased after 1828 when the western Cherokees exchanged their Arkansas reservation for the "Lovely Purchase" and began large-scale emigration to what is now eastern Oklahoma. This exodus conformed to the general Indian policy that President Andrew Jackson instituted in 1830. Jackson called for forcible removal of all aboriginal Americans to the territory west of Missouri and Arkansas. Where the Arkansas Osages had once been challenged only by factions of the Cherokees and other eastern tribes, they soon found resident in their domain thousands of new emigrants — Choctaw, Chickasaw, Creek, Seminoles and Cherokees.

42

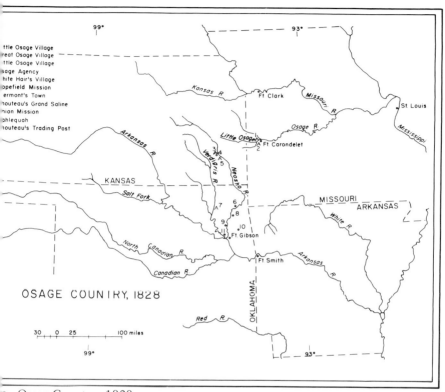

ttle Osage Village
reat Osage Village
ttle Osage Village
sage Agency
hite Hair's Village
apefield Mission
ermont's Town
houteau's Grand Saline
nion Mission
ahlequah
houteau's Trading Post

OSAGE COUNTRY, 1828

30   0   25        100 miles

2. Osage Country, 1828.

Incapable of fighting all of the newcomers, Clermont's people had to come to terms if they were to survive. Thus, in treaties negotiated in May, 1831, the Arkansas Osages agreed to a cessation of hostilities with both the Cherokees and the Creeks, but they refused to remove to the Kansas reservation.

Their determination to remain compounded problems arising from Jackson's removal policy. How could the Cherokees and Creeks be re-settled if some of the Little Ones occupied the land? To deal with the problem, a special presidential commission headed by Gov. Montfort Stokes of North Carolina met the Osages at Chouteau's trading house at the Grand Saline in February, 1833. Yet extensive preparations by Col. Couteau and lengthy discourses by the commissioners could not persuade the Arkansas Osages to join their kinsmen in Kansas.

To underscore their independence, a war party of 300 led by Clermont the younger (the elder died in 1828) set out to renew hostilities with their traditional enemies on the Plains. In due time they viciously attacked a defenseless Kiowa village located in the Washita Mountains. Killing at least 150 men, women and children, they took several prisoners and stole the tribe's horses. The victory resembled the exploits of an older, perhaps better day.

If the refusal of the Arkansas Osages to

remove to Kansas created a problem for the United States, their attack upon the Kiowas presented an even more serious one. Such a bloody expedition might incite a general Plains Indian retaliation against the eastern emigrants, seriously jeopardizing the removal policy. To repair the damages, Col. Henry Dodge in June, 1834, led 500 dragoons and a contingent of Osages and emigrant Indians to the Washita Mountains. After returning the captives taken by the Little Ones the previous year, Dodge induced representatives of the Kiowa, Comanche and Wichita tribes to accompany the expedition back to Fort Gibson. A three-day conclave followed with Osage, Cherokee, Creek and Choctaw delegates. Instead of encouraging a formal treaty, however, the United States used the occasion to plan another conference to be held the following year on the Plains where the western tribes could participate more easily.

The pre-arranged convocation occurred at Camp Holmes near present Lexington, Oklahoma, in July, 1835. Eight thousand Kiowa and Comanches gathered to "talk" with eighty Osages and equally large delegations from the emigrant tribes. Gov. Stokes and Gen. Arbuckle represented the interests of the United States. On August 24, after lengthy discussions, most of the tribes agreed to a treaty of peace and good will, and the Plains Indians guaranteed their eastern neighbors the right to hunt and trap on their domain.

The Kiowas and the Osages did not sign the Camp Holmes Treaty. The Kiowas had old scores to settle before making peace; the Little Ones feared that their signatures would bring their removal to Kansas.

Still, the removal of the Arkansas Osages from the Verdigris was only a matter of time. Suspicious and resentful, their Indian neighbors depleted the game upon which the band depended for sustenance. Decimated by cholera in 1834 and leaderless after the death of Clermont the younger in 1837, the Arkansas Osage succumbed to the inevitable and at Fort Gibson relinquished their Verdigris River homes on January 11, 1839. As compensation, the United States paid them $20,000 in money and provisions, furnished agricultural supplies and assumed all claims against them up to $30,000. After Gen. Arbuckle sent his dragoons to insure their removal, the Clermont band left its villages and moved north to join elements of the tribe already in Kansas.

Restricted to a reservation after 1839, the Little Ones were not a broken or dissipated people. They were men supreme, still confident in the efficacy of their cultural system and their faith in *Wa-kon-da*. Vigorous assaults upon their traditions had made few inroads. Indeed, two

Protestant missions established among them by 1821 had failed. These included Union Mission, located one mile west of the Neosho River in modern Mayes County, Oklahoma, and Harmony Mission, situated on the Marais des Cygnes in present Bates County, Missouri. Hopefield, a subsidiary mission, was established in 1823 five miles north of Union and re-established in 1828 near Cabin Creek. It too was unsuccessful. Sponsored by the American Board of Commissioners for Foreign Missions, all three mission efforts were disbanded by 1837.

Several factors accounted for the failures. While the constant prospect of war suppressed any interest in Union Mission, the removal of the Osages from Missouri in 1822 retarded development of Harmony Mission. Also, the Osages had no real interest in the white man's God. Though White Hair had held the "Black Book" in reverence, the elder Clermont proved indifferent to the gospel. Finally, the Osages spurned the educational opportunities provided by the missions. In 11 years only 71 Osage children took instruction at Union, and after 12 years only 133 enrolled at Harmony. Though the Little Ones responded more positively to the efforts of Father Charles Quickenbourne, the Catholic missions were as unsuccessful as the Protestant. Obviously, for the Little Ones *Wa-kon-da* still reigned as sovereign.

## ON THE KANSAS RESERVATION, 1839 TO 1871

By collecting the Osages on the Kansas reservation, the United States had hoped to facilitate peaceful relations between the emigrants and resident tribes. The eastern intruder, though, continued to find the displaced aboriginals less than hospitable. Inasmuch as a meeting of the minds seemed essential, in the 1840's the emigrants resorted to direct diplomacy and invited the Osages and other resident Indians to a series of inter-tribal councils. In May, 1842, the Creeks presided over a conclave near present Eufaula, Oklahoma. In June of the next year, Cherokee Chief John Ross convened a council at Tahlequah, attended by 3000 to 4000 representatives of at least 23 tribes. The Creeks hosted still another convention at Okmulgee in late 1843 and two more in 1845, one on Deep Fork River and the other on the Salt Plains. Though these conclaves generally produced treaties of friendship, the participation of the Little Ones was never enthusiastic. Surprisingly, they had developed interests elsewhere.

On the reserve the Osages had turned their attention to developing harmonious relationships with western Indian tribes. Indeed, they had negotiated a military alliance with the Comanches, the Kiowas, and the Apaches.

Courtesy Mrs. Villa Tinker Hill

GEN. CLARENCE LEONARD TINKER, U. S. AIR CORPS. Maj. Gen. Tinker, son of
ge E. and Sarah Anna (Nan) Tinker, assumed command of the Pacific Ocean Air
s and the Hawaiian Air Force at Hickam Field, Hawaii, in December, 1941. In
, 1942 he was killed in action during the Battle of Midway. Tinker Air Force
in Oklahoma City is named for Maj. Gen. Tinker, (photo was taken December,
, shortly after Tinker took command in Hawaii).

Though detractors accused the Little Ones of planning a combined attack upon the emigrant Indians, the new orientation was in fact more commercial than military.

Building upon the good will generated at Camp Holmes, the Osages had instituted a vigorous and profitable trade with the Comanches. From Melicourt Papin, representative of the American Fur Trading Company, and John Mathews, an entrepreneur who had purchased the Chouteau interests, they secured guns, blankets, powder and lead. Taking the merchandise to the Salt Plains of northwest Oklahoma, the Little Ones exchanged it with the Comanches for mules. In 1847 alone they bartered $24,000 worth of trade goods for 1500 mules valued at $60,000. The Osage-Comanche trade continued until 1855 when annuities provided by the government made the Plains Indians independent of the manufactured items previously furnished by the Osages.

In addition to insuring its removal policy, the United States assembled the Little Ones in Kansas presumably to protect the tribe from the vices and greed of the white men. Though an honest objective, it proved impossible to attain. American citizens early and frequently cross the reservation as a result of commerce on the Santa Fe Trail. Intrusions increased during the course of the Mexican War and following the discovery of gold in California. The Osages met these trespassers who indiscriminately slaughtered the buffalo as they met the red intruders — by attack after attack. Indeed the assults were so disrupting that the government in 1855 assigned two regiments to patrol the Plains. Though the troopers prevented retaliations, they only facilitated the violation of the tribal borders.

By contrast, the Little Ones welcomed some white men. In April, 1847, they permitted Father John Schoenmakers to establish a Catholic Mission on the Neosho River near modern St. Paul, Kansas. The following month Fr. Schoenmakers opened the Osage Manual Laboratory School, enrolling 28 students during the first year. Assisted by the Sisters of Loretto and Father Paul Ponsiglione, he gradually enlarged the school so that 136 boys and 100 girls attended daily classes in 1860. Also, the Catholic missionaries had some success in attracting converts to the Holy Faith, a reflection of the esteem rendered these dedicated men.

If the Santa Fe Trail and mission efforts brought hundreds of white men to the Osage reservation, the passage of the Kansas-Nebraska Act in 1854 brought thousands. Abolitionists and proslave settlers poured into Kansas Territory, and though most stopped at the borders of the reserve some took up residence in the very midst of the Little Ones, insisting upon the right of agriculturalists to displace hunters. Some even

51

sought to involve the tribe in the emotional issue of slavery. John Mathews, for example, espoused the southern view, while Fr. Schoenmakers supported the abolitionist cause. Unaware of the subtleties of the question, the Osages divided on the slavery issue according to their personal loyalties.

The divisive issue that carried the United States to Civil War in April, 1861, also brought war to the Little Ones. To protect their western flank and insure much needed allies, the Southern States commissioned Albert Pike, an Arkansas attorney, to negotiate treaties of alliance with those tribes in Indian Territory. By September, 1861, Pike had entered into conventions with all of the tribes save for the Cherokees, the Quapaws, the Senecas and Shawnees and the Osages. In October at Tahlequah these nations accepted a Confederate alliance and agreed to become parties to the existing war. The Osage delegation, however, was not unanimous in its commitment to the southern cause. Led by Striking Axe, the Little Ones refused to sign Pike's treaty, a reluctance that proved to be the more popular view. Back in Kansas most of the Great Osages also repudiated the Tahlequah accord with only the Black Dog and Clermont bands remaining loyal to the South. As in the past, the white man had again divided the ancient house of the Little Ones.

A number of Osages actively supported the

military effort of the Union. Little Bear and other Little Osages joined the Ninth Kansas Infantry while a number of White Hair's people attached themselves to the Union troops at Fort Scott. Two hundred Osages led by Chetopa mustered into the Second Regiment of the Indian Brigade, but their services proved less than spectacular. Recruited in June, 1862, to participate in Weer's raid on Tahlequah, Chetopa's company deserted as a body before the expedition got to Indian Territory. But the Little Ones made up for this indiscretion. In May, 1863, they intercepted a party of some 22 Confederate officers on their way to Colorado, forced them to make a stand on the upper Verdigris River and then utterly decimated them. The assault made the tribe heroes in the eyes of Kansas authorities. W. S. Coffin, agent of the Osages, even permitted some of Black Dog's people to return unhindered to the reservation despite their sympathy with the Confederacy.

Largely on the periphery of actual combat, the tribe nevertheless was significantly affected by the Civil War. Its reservation was criss-crossed by both northern and southern partisans, and it was inundated by refugees streaming out of Indian Territory. More importantly, the war provided the occasion for Kansas authorities to demand that the Little Ones cede a portion of their domain for white development. These entreaties culminated in August, 1863, when

53

Commissioner of Indian Affairs William P. Dole pressured the tribal leadership into relinquishing tracts along the eastern and northern edges of the reservation. Dole, however, negotiated without the presence of the tribal rank and file, who, upon learning the terms of the proposed treaty, quickly disavowed it. This, along with opposition in the United States Senate, prevented final ratification of the agreement.

The seeds of cession, once sown, could not escape a harvest. Following a Fort Smith conference where the southern Indians, including an Osage contingent, ended their "rebellion," United States authorities again assembled the Little Ones at Canville's Trading Post on the Neosho River. On September 29, 1865, the tribe consented to a treaty similar to the one signed with Dole two years earlier. They agreed to cede the eastern 30 miles of their reservation and to sell a 20-mile-wide tract that extended the entire distance of their northern boundary. The tribe also pledged to remove from the relinquished territory within six months. As compensation, the government promised to pay $300,000 for the eastern segment and to sell the northern cession for not less than $1.25 per acre. The net proceeds of the sale, along with the $300,000, would be placed in a tribal trust fund.

The Osages, of course, had been guaranteed perpetual use of their entire Kansas reserve in 1825. Nevertheless, the United States insisted upon the 1865 cession, rationalizing it as necessary to protect the Little Ones from the corrupt influence of the white man. Also, the new treaty would chastise the tribe for "joining" the Confederacy. In actual fact Kansas residents coveted the tribal domain. As the government could not or would not impede the greed of its citizens, it simply accommodated it.

The situation did not improve on the Diminished Reservation. When the Osages returned from their spring and autumn buffalo hunts they often found their dwellings and fields occupied by belligerent white men. This ceaseless invasion of their homes along with increasingly unsuccessful hunts brought the tribal leadership to agree to additional talks with the government. In May, 1868, President Andrew Johnson sent commissioners and 30 soldiers of the Seventh Cavalry to meet the Osages at Drum Creek. After the usual pleasantries the federal officials proposed a treaty whereby the Little Ones would sell their remaining reserve of 8,000,000 acres to the Leavenworth, Lawrence and Galveston Railway for $1,600,000. The tribe would then use the proceeds of the sale to purchase a new home in Indian Territory where the government could better protect them. But the Osages had been "protected" before, and they balked at accepting the proposed treaty of cession.

An unanticipated event brought the Little

Ones to a more favorable view. A party of 360 warriors returned to the council grounds with two scalps they claimed to have lifted from Arapahoes. But a young white man charged that the scalps were those of his brother and friend, and he and other whites threatened the Osages with immediate reprisals. Aware that the Seventh Cavalry stood by, the Little Ones were thoroughly frightened. When the commissioners conveniently promised to quiet the settlers, they signed the so-called Sturges Treaty (after the President of the benefited railroad) on May 27, 1868.

Once their hysteria cooled, Kansas citizens learned the true meaning of the agreement. Eight million fertile acres had been passed to the ownership of a railroad corporation, a fact that would deprive them at least of modestly priced homesteads. Kansas Gov. S. J. Crawford made the "dispossession" his special cause, and when Congress listened, President U. S. Grant withdrew the document from further congressional consideration.

Yet the presidential action only proved a reprieve. Grant's "Peace Policy" could not maintain the integrity of the Diminished Reservation. White men consistently stole Osage horses, abused tribal hunting parties and crassly settled on the reserve. Organized into claims clubs, they surveyed "their" land, set off town sites and established counties. One county even voted a

$200,000 bond issue to entice a railroad to its borders.

Unable or unwilling to preserve the Little Ones in their Kansas reservation, the federal government finally legalized the dispossession then occurring. On July 15, 1870, Congress directed that the Osage Diminished Reserve be sold for $1.25 per acre and that the net proceeds of the sale be placed to the credit of the Indians at 5% interest. Congress also authorized the tribe to use the funds to purchase a new home in Indian Territory.

Since implementation of the legislation required the consent of the Osages, President Grant in August, 1870, sent the Board of Indian Commissioners to council with the tribe at Drum Creek. Again returned from an unsuccessful hunt to homes pre-empted by whites, the Osages accepted the inevitable and agreed to the basic provisions of the congressional act. Later, they demanded and received more land than initially assigned them in Indian Territory, protection from trespassers, partial control of the tribal trust fund, ownership of land in common, and the right to hunt buffalo on the Plains.

The same council that consented to the sale of the Diminished Reserve also appointed a delegation to select the new tribal home. On October 26, 1870, the chiefs decided upon a location near modern Bartlesville, Oklahoma, an area to which the Cherokees had relinquished title in 1866. Elements of the tribe immediately settled the region, began improvements, cultivated the land and planted crops.

Federal officials soon determined that the initial settlements were erroneously located and must be moved further west. As compensation for the error, the government agreed to increase the size of the new reserve to include 1.7 million acres lying west of the 96th meridian, south of the Kansas state line, and north and east of the Arkansas River. The Osages consented to pay $1,099,137.41, (70c per acre) for the tract out of the $10,000,000 received for their Kansas estate. The payment left approximately $8.5 million in tribal trust fund.

By mid-1872 nearly 4000 Osages with 12,000 horses had settled in Indian Territory. The five physical divisions of the tribe established themselves on terrain similar to that which their ancestors had fled at the time of the Great Flood. White Hair's band located south of modern Pawhuska, Oklahoma, and Saucy Chief's people just north. Clermont's folk established themselves near present Hominy. Striking Axe's Little Osages settled in the northeastern corner of the reservation on Mission Creek, and "Governor Joe's" Big Hills near modern Grey Horse. With the selection of these sites, the Little Ones finally chose what in actual fact became their permanent homes.

58

# IN INDIAN TERRITORY,
## 1872 TO 1907

The removal to Indian Territory did not initially alter the traditional economic and social patterns of the Little Ones. The spring and autumn buffalo hunts to the Plains occurred with the regularity of the changing seasons. Successful hunts, however, were more the exception than the rule because the bison herds were systematically destroyed by white hunters. With their life source threatened, the Plains tribes launched attack after attack upon those American citizens who violated their domain. The depredations brought swift retaliation from the United States government who in the mid-1870's declared war on the belligerent tribes. Though the Little Ones were not participants in the so-called Red River War, they were affected by it. In the summer of 1874 a party of 29 Osages established a hunting camp on Medicine Lodge Creek within the boundaries of their old Kansas reservation. Just as they prepared to return to Indian Territory, a party of whites killed four of them and robbed the remainder of their meat, robes, kettles and horses.

The unwarranted attack brought the Little Ones to the verge of war with the United States. That the Osages did not join the hostile Plains Indians was due to the decisive action taken by

Isaac Gibson, the Osage agent. Upon learning of the Medicine Lodge Creek murders, he simultaneously dispatched supplies and wagons to the desolate party and demanded that Kansas authorities prosecute the guilty whites. He also sent runners to other hunting parties on the Plains and requested them to remain calm and return immediately to the reservation.

Back at the agency the Little Ones learned that the Kansas governor refused to punish those guilty for the recent massacre. Indeed, he mustered the killers into the militia and then backdated their papers so that the malicious attack appeared as official business. So fearful was Gibson that the governor's response would bring the Osages to join the Plains tribes that in the fall of 1874 he requested that troops be sent to the agency. The arrival of the Fifth Cavalry from Fort Sill, along with a trip of tribal leaders to Lawrence, Kansas, to counsel with federal officials, stilled the troubled waters. Yet the traditional lifeways of the Little Ones would never be the same: the buffalo were gone and hunting trips were hazardous.

With the cessation of the traditional hunts, every aspect of reservation life became increasingly important to the Osages. Of special concern was what happened at the agency. Established in 1872 at modern Pawhuska, the agency consisted of buildings that were initially log but later permanent, sandstone structures.

60

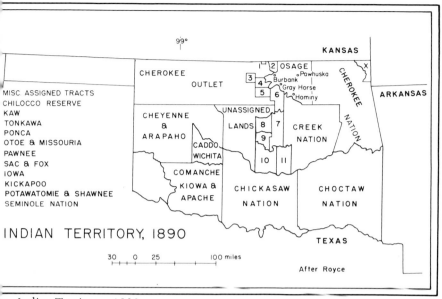

MISC ASSIGNED TRACTS
CHILOCCO RESERVE
KAW
TONKAWA
PONCA
OTOE & MISSOURIA
PAWNEE
SAC & FOX
IOWA
KICKAPOO
POTAWATOMIE & SHAWNEE
SEMINOLE NATION

KANSAS

CHEROKEE
OUTLET

OSAGE
Pawhuska
Burbank
Gray Horse
Hominy

CHEROKEE NATION

ARKANSAS

CHEYENNE
&
ARAPAHO

UNASSIGNED
LANDS

CADDO
WICHITA

CREEK
NATION

COMANCHE

KIOWA &
APACHE

CHICKASAW
NATION

CHOCTAW
NATION

INDIAN TERRITORY, 1890

TEXAS

30  0  25          100 miles

After Royce

3. Indian Territory, 1890.

61

The several-acre compound was remarkable for its commotion and activity, particularly at quarterly annuity payments and during the issuance of rations. Of all the tribal agents who presided at Pawhuska, Maj. Laban J. Miles of Iowa was by far the most capable and highly respected. A sensitive, sympathetic and dedicated man, he could also be stern and uncompromising, especially in his use of Indian police. Yet in a service that spanned two decades, Miles won the lasting affection of the tribe.

Another aspect of reservation life important to the Little Ones was the commerce transacted with traders and trading houses. Firms such as Dunlap and Florer as well as Hiatt and Company initially bartered for the buffalo hides collected on the bi-annual hunts. In 1874 alone the traders took in 10,800 robes valued at $60,000. After the hunts ceased in 1876, the merchants simply stocked the manufactured items desired by the Osages. Purchasing the goods on credit, the Indians recorded the amount of indebtedness by notches on a stick. On annuity days when money was distributed per capita the Little Ones repaid the traders. Business with the Osages was so profitable that by the 1890's as many as 21 individuals had been licensed to engage in commerce with them.

Educational activity was still another significant feature of reservation life. In 1872 Isaac

Gibson opened a government boarding school at the agency and enrolled 90 students by the end of the year. The school provided instruction in traditional courses and a one-hundred acre demonstration farm. At first excluded from the reservation by Gibson, the Catholics also established two educational institutions following a special act by the Osage national council in 1887. Staffed by one of several teaching orders of nuns, St. Louis School for Girls at Pawhuska and St. John's School for Boys at Grey Horse accommodated more than 100 students. More advanced Osage students attended schools in the states, especially Osage Manual Labor School at St. Paul, Kansas, and Haskell Institute at Lawrence, Kansas, but also Carlisle Indian School in Pennsylvania and Hampton Institute in Virginia.

Though traditional spiritual concepts were changing, religious life on the reservation retained its importance. By the 1870's *Wa-kon-da* seemed impotent to the Osages. That which he had provided as the staff of life, the buffalo, was gone; his people had been pushed from place to place. As the death of the bison and the loss of their land was caused by the white man, the Little Ones rationalized that the Christian God must be the more powerful.

This significant conclusion had different ramifications. Some of the Osages sought to compromise the old with the new. Combining elements of the Indian's spirit world with the concept of Christ as the tortured son of God, they fashioned the theology of the Native American Church. Using peyote as a sacrament, the church provided a religious blend significantly different but not completely severed from the old way.

Other Little Ones rejected a spiritual compromise and embraced traditional forms of Christianity. For a time the Quakers had a religious monopoloy among the Osages as the Grant Peace Policy envisioned only one denomination at each reservation. Under the guidance of Agent Gibson, the Society of Friends conducted Sunday schools, mission efforts and worship services. Yet the Friends were never as successful as the Catholics. Continuous religious instruction and educational opportunities made the Osages a "Catholic Tribe."

Reservation life also brought changes in the tribal organization. By 1880 the Little Ones recognized the Grand Peace Chief and the Grand War Chief only as chieftains of one of their physical divisions. Indeed, after the so-called Sturges Treaty in 1868 when he was appointed as Governor of all the Osages, Big Hill Joe assumed the role as principal spokesman for the tribe. As Joe's leadership was never wholly satisfactory, Agent Laban Miles urged the tribe to institute a democratic form of government.

64

On December 31, 1881, James Bigheart led the Osages in adopting a constitution that was patterned after that of the Cherokees. The document provided for a national council, a principal chief and an assistant chief, and a judicial system of supreme, circuit and lower courts. Each of five designated districts elected a sheriff and three delegates to the national council. The two chiefs were elected at large, while the council selected the judges of the different courts. All officers served two-year terms. Though the constitution was never approved by federal authorities, it established a semi-official government that enacted such useful legislation as compulsory education for tribal youngsters.

The governmental system also provided a forum for the various factions within the tribe. Political parties were organized: the mixed-bloods fashioned a "Progressive Party" and the full bloods formed a conservative coalition. Debate over mineral leases, allotment of lands, legitimacy of the tribal roll, and the influence of the agent was vigorous and divisive. For that matter, it was so acrimonious that after the disputed elections in 1898 and 1900 the tribal agent abolished the national council. The office of chief, however, was continued.

Besides altering their government form, the reservation brought alterations in the economic life of the Little Ones. The rolling terrain of the tribal domain, with its cover of blackjack oak and bluestem grass, did not encourage agriculture, and the Osages relied initially for sustenance upon the buffalo hunt; after 1876 they had to make do with rations issued by the agency at Pawhuska. Each Osage also drew an annual per capita payment of about $200, a sum derived from interest accrued on the trust fund.

Agricultural leases provided another source of revenue. A tribal member frequently selected a site on the reservation as his own and leased it as a farming location to a white emigrant. By the turn of the century the average Osage had from one to six farms leased in this fashion. Likewise, the national council granted similar leases, but on a larger scale, to white cattlemen. Tom Wagoner, owner of the famous 3-D Ranch and the renowned Texas rancher, at one time grazed 15,000 head on Osage land. By 1893 more than one-half of the reservation, or 831,000 acres, had been leased to grazing interests, a practice that by 1906 brought revenue to the tribe totalling $98,376. The grazing leases, though obviously important economically, also had strategic value. Located in the northern portion of the reservation, they provided a buffer against any greedy Kansas homesteader who might desire to displace the Little Ones again. Settlers always thought twice before they plowed up some rancher's lease.

Prior to 1907 royalties accruing from oil and

gas extraction also provided the Osages with a modest income. That deliverable quantities of oil and gas lay beneath the surface of the reservation had long been known. To tap these resources, Chief James Bigheart in March, 1896, executed a ten-year blanket lease for the whole of the reserve with Phoenix Oil Company founded by Edwin B. Foster. The company brought in its first well in October, 1896, but financial setbacks caused its reorganization in December, 1901, when it assumed the name of Indian Territory Illuminating Oil Company. The reorganized company granted numerous subleases to stimulate exploration, an action that resulted in the drilling of 361 wells by the end of 1904. Even at that, these wells represented only a fraction of those later completed.

For a time after their removal to Indian Territory, the Little Ones successfully isolated themselves from the land-hungry white man who had forced them from their Kansas reservation. Yet the ever-westward movement of the American nation made permanent isolation impossible, particularly after the opening of Oklahoma Territory in 1889 and the Cherokee Strip in 1893. Equally ominous for the Little Ones was the policy adopted by the United States in 1887 whereby Indians were allotted 160 acre plots and the "surplus" portions of their reservations opened to white settlement. When Congress exempted the Osages from both the Dawes and

Curtis Acts, measures were taken to secure tribal approval of a special allotment program. In 1893 the government sent the Cherokee Allotment Commission and the following year a special Osage commission to instruct the Little Ones on the advantages of private property. Neither, however, gained consent to an allotted reservation.

Several reasons explained the failure. James Bigheart and Black Dog, for example, noted that, like Indians of other tribes, the Osages might very well lose their allotments after the dissolution of the reserve. Landless, the Little Ones would be completely at the mercy of the government. As traditional allotment procedures vested surface and sub-surface rights in the allotee, they also argued that breaking up the reservation would enrich the few at the expense of the many. Revenue derived from oil and gas deposits would go only to those who owned the well site instead of the whole tribe. Further, Bigheart insisted that the tribal roll which would serve as the basis for allotment listed families who were not Osages and not entitled to share in the tribal estate. When the Bureau of Indian Affairs retained on the roll the names challenged by Bigheart, the full bloods' opposition to allotment was confirmed.

Still, among the Little Ones there was considerable support for dissolving the reservation. The mixed-bloods saw allotment as an

ЗE COUNCIL 1895. Council members were Jno. Mosier — interpreter; White
ι; Ne-kah-wah-she-tun-kah; Gov. Bigheart; Pete Casey; W. T. Leahey; Joe
ιanger; Che-sho-hun-kah; Clatemore; Black Dog O-lo-hah-wah-la; A-she-gah-hre;
no-hah; Julian Trumbly; Saucy Chief; Chas. Prudom; and Mo-she-to-moig.

opportunity to manage their own affairs and to attain a status equal to that of the white man. Their view became the majority view when they surpassed the full bloods in the population count. Furthermore, the mixed-bloods concluded that division of the tribal estate was inevitable, especially after Congress authorized the construction of railroads across the reservation, established five townsites, and designated that the reserve should become a county when Oklahoma became a state. There could be no question as to allotment after March, 1904, when Bird S. McGuire, the congressional delegate of the Territory, introduced the necessary legislation.

So significant was tribal support for allotment that in June, 1904, the Osages elected as chief the candidate that favored the action. An allotment bill was drafted and approved by the tribe in a subsequent general election. In February, 1906, the measure was taken to Washington by an Osage delegation representing all factions of the tribe, and by June it had received congressional approval.

The Osage Allotment Act differed from similar acts in that it reserved all mineral rights to the tribe, a provision championed largely by James Bigheart. It also directed that the entire reservation would be divided among enrolled Osages, with one 160-acre tract designated as a homestead and restricted against alienation for

70

25 years. There would be no "surplus" land available for white men, though under certain conditions the individual might sell that portion of his allotment not restricted. Directing that the tribal trust fund should be divided among enrolled members and credited to individual accounts, the allotment act also called for the creation of a new tribal council.

To carry out the provisions of the legislation, the United States appointed a commission of three members, one a fullblood Osage. First establishing a tribal roll that listed 2229 Osages, the commission allotted 658 acres to each enrolled member, making every effort to locate the entire allotment in the same general area. It also apportioned the tribal trust fund among the allotees, assigning each $3819.

Simultaneously with the adoption of the allotment act, Congress passed the Oklahoma Enabling Act. It too was important to the Osages, authorizing as it did an Oklahoma constitutional convention of 55 delegates from Indian Territory, 55 delegates from Oklahoma Territory, and two from the Osage nation. In elections held on November 5, 1906, Democrats T. J. Leady and J. S. Quarles were selected as the Osage representatives. In late November all delegates assembled in Guthrie, where they wrote a constitution ultimately adopted by the residents of the Territory. Oklahoma entered the Union one year later on November 16, 1907.

71

With their lands allotted and their reserve an Oklahoma county, the Little Ones no longer existed as an independent people.

## INTO THE TWENTIETH CENTURY

Alterations in the tribal life of the Osages occurred throughout the 20th Century, but none was as dramatic as the alternation of their economy. Recipients of a modest income from trust funds and agriculture leases at the time of allotment, by 1920 the Little Ones were the wealthiest people in the world. The exploitation of mineral resources on the tribal reserve explained the development.

In 1906 when the original Foster "blanket lease" expired, a new 10-year lease on 680,000 acres was granted to the Indian Territory Illuminating Oil Company. Though the company, which continued to be dominant in the reserve until it merged with Cities Service Oil Company in 1941, agreed to royalty increases from one-tenth to one-eighth, it did not pay a bonus for specific leases. As such a payment on proven oil reserves was common, parties in Oklahoma, especially Gov. Charles Haskell, hinted of political favoritism and corruption. The lease stood as executed, however, and the I. T. I. O. Company and its subleasees continued profitable exploitation of "The Osage."

The successful production of oil made those acres not yet under lease even more attractive to

72

competing corporations. For a time they submitted sealed bids through the Department of the Interior, offering cash bonuses to the tribe for the right to develop specified leases. As these offers were usually small, the Osage council instituted a system of public auctions where particular tracts were leased to those who paid the highest bonus. The first such auction was held at Pawhuska on November 11, 1912; during the succeeding 15 years 28 more occurred.

Col. E. E. Walters presided over these "Osage Monte Carlos" held under a large elm tree near the agency. At the first auction he disposed of 107,000 acres for a bonus of $39,000, approximately 37c per acre. Ten years later, after the development of the Burbank field, he sold a third as much acreage for bonuses aggregating $10 million or nearly $300 per acre. The Gypsy Oil Company purchased one 160-acre tract for $1,600,000, but the record bonus was paid two years later in May, 1924 when the Skelly-Phillips combination paid $1,990,000 for a similar lease. On that day bonuses paid aggregated $14 million.

Though the bonuses paid by the various firms were fantastic, they amounted to only a fraction of the oil royalties received by the Little Ones. Between 1907 and 1929, the tribe received $233,000,000 in royalties and bonuses. By 1957, an additional $167,000,000 had been received, and by 1971 at least $100,000,000

73

more. Altogether, "the Osage" has generated more than $511,481,402 in revenue for the tribe.

The sums received as royalties and bonus payments were credited on a per capita basis to the individual accounts or divided among the heirs of each of the original 2229 allotees. Known as a "headright," these payments amounted to $384 in 1916, to $3762 in 1918, and to $8090 in 1920. The largest payment occurred in 1925 when $13,200 was credited to each headright. By 1929 every allotted Osage had netted over $102,534 from oil royalties. The amount paid plummetted in 1932 to $585, but rose in 1943 to $1120 and increased to $1905 in 1952. In 1970 the headright payment was $2780.

Tremendously wealthy, the Little Ones were frequently extravagant and reckless in the use of their funds. With "an Olympian attitude toward money," one Osage lady in a single afternoon in 1927 purchased a $12,000 fur coat, a $3000 diamond ring, a $5000 automobile, $7000 in furniture which she shipped to California for another $600, and made a $4000 down payment on a California home and a $12,800 investment in Florida real estate. Another fullblood allotee who received $86,142 in headright payments between 1916 and 1926 had nothing to show for it by the latter date but a car valued at $350 on which he still owed $400.

74

LEO MILES (left, 1894-1950) and Charley Whip (right, 1864-1937) had fine cars, but neither had any driving experience. Their housekeeper (center) had to le as their chauffeur.

In many instances unscrupulous white men accounted for much of the wild spending and dissipation of funds. Lawyers addicted to sharp practices had themselves designated guardians of Osages declared incompetent by the County Court. In control of his ward's wealth, the attorney then manipulated it to his own advantage. One such "guardian" purchased an automobile for $250 and then sold it to his ward for $1250. As business manager of another Indian, this same attorney conducted his client's affairs so that by 1929 he was in debt approximately $20,000 for mortgages held by his attorney. This indebtedness occurred despite the fact that within the year the Osage had inherited an estate valued at more than $90,000 and since 1921 had been receiving $7000 to $12,000 annually. The record is replete with shenanigans of this type. Additionally, Osage county lawyers always demanded and frequently received gigantic fees for representing Indians in cases before the courts. In one divorce action that took no more than 20 minutes before the judge, attorneys for both parties received fees of $1000 each.

Some medical doctors and merchants were just as unscrupulous. Several physicians made practices of ministering to wealthy Osages. In 1952 one charged an elderly woman a fee of $6115 which included a $6.00 daily charge for a night call, an additional charge for a second

DE OF OWNERSHIP"

home or office call, and three dollars per day for medications. In that year he was paid a total of $14,372 for services to 22 restricted Indians. Another physician received $24,017 for services to 34 restricted Osages. Similarily, local merchants enticed wealthy Indians to buy everything from expensive automobiles (such as a Pierce Arrow) to photographs and picture albums. These items were frequently purchased on credit despite the immense payments made to individual Osages and contrary to instructions issued by the tribal agent. In June, 1922, 194 such debts totalled $817,523, interest on a part of which was charged at 10% per quarter.

In addition to the shady practices of some "friends," the wealth of the Little Ones attracted criminal elements to the Osage reserve, instituting what contemporary observers labeled as the "Osage Reign of Terror." Al Spencer's notorious gang of outlaws operated in the county, as did Henry Grammer, the celebrated "King of the Bootleggers." But these and others of lesser repute were small frys compared to W. K. Hale.

Between 1921 and 1923 several members of one prominent family died under mysterious circumstances. In July, 1921, Lizzie Q. Brown, an aged Osage woman, passed away leaving her eight headrights to three daughters. The following spring, one daughter, Anna, was found dead of a gunshot wound in the head. A few weeks

later, authorities discovered the body of her
ex-brother-in-law, Henry Roan. And in May,
1923, Anna's sister, Mrs. W. E. Smith, and her
family perished in a dynamite blast that completely destroyed their home. Accordingly, the
whole Brown fortune of more than $100,000
per year passed to Molly, the surviving sister
who was also the wife of Ernest Buckhart, the
nephew of W. K. Hale.

Initially, Osage County officials manifested
little interest in the murders. After spending
$20,000 of its own funds, the tribal council
finally induced federal investigators to enter the
case. Evidence was gathered and charges
ultimately filed against Hale, Burkhart and their
accomplices. The trials revealed that Hale had
masterminded the plot, even collecting a
$25,000 insurance policy on Roan, and that
Burkhart had procured the assassins who had
perpetrated the murders. Conviction finally
came at the conclusion of the second trial, after
which the reign of terror in the Osage nation
terminated. Yet for the Little Ones the era was
not soon forgotten. Some had left the county,
others armed themselves, and still others strung
lights about their homes to thwart would-be
murderers.

The reckless spending, corruption and
criminal activity attendant to Osage wealth
convinced the federal government that careful
supervision was necessary if the tribe were to

THE OSAGE INDIAN, confronted with his new found "headright" wealth, paradoxi
spurned the architecture and other domestic innovations of the whitema
evidenced in this photograph, but – at the same time, "the little ones"

tten with and quickly adopted the metal horses of transportation that came
ring out of Detroit and became a permanent part of life on the Osage reservation!

retain any of its wealth. In May, 1921, Congress ended the practice of immediately paying out to the headright owners all that was received in bonus and royalty payments. Instead, it directed that allotted Osages not having certificates of competency should receive quarterly stipends of only $1000 with an additional $500 for the support of minor children. Those funds accruing above and beyond the quarterly payment — labeled "surplus funds" — were to be invested in United States bonds and various types of state bonds or placed on time deposit in local banks. After February, 1925, these surplus monies could be expended for the benefit of the individual upon approval of the Secretary of the Interior. Such belated arrangements brought some conservation of funds.

Careful federal supervision, however, did not apply to all of the Little Ones. The Osage Allotment Act had provided that those allotees judged capable of managing their own affairs should be given certificates of competency. Such certificates in effect removed all special government restrictions on the Indian except for his interest in the tribal mineral estate and his 160-acre homestead allotment. Under terms of the act, some 1164 certificates were issued, a number increased by legislation passed in March, 1929. The latter measure directed the issuance of certificates to all allotted adults of less than one-half Indian blood. Finally in 1948 Congress provided that those Osages not at least one-half Indian blood should be certified as competent upon reaching 21 years of age. Accordingly, by 1952, 2390 members of the tribe, or 79% of all adults, had been issued certificates of competency. To that total 2691 more had been added 20 years later.

Initially, a competency certificate did not permit alienation of the 160-acre homestead allotment. Legislation in 1921 and 1948, however, removed that restriction upon those Little Ones with less than one-half Indian blood. Once certified as to competency, the Osages usually sold their land: by 1957 the surface rights to 1.1 of the 1.4 million acre reservation had been alienated. But restructions upon those properties — both real estate and royalty payments — owned by Osages of more than one-half Indian blood have been continued, first to 1959, then to 1984, and recently until Congress sees fit to remove them. This restriction also applies to the tribe's vested interest in the total mineral estate.

The issuance of an increasing number of certificates of competency indicates that the majority of the Osages have severed themselves from any federal government restrictions. In 1952, for example, only 14% of the total tribal population had trust accounts at the Osage agency. For better or for worse, most of the Little Ones are as independent of federal

BUSTLING DOWNTOWN PAWHUSKA, OKLAHOMA, capital of the Osage Nation,
holiday in the 1920's, complete with flags and traffic jam. When the exploitati
Osage oil resources began in 1907, "allotted" tribal members (those between v
the reservation was divided by the Osage Allotment Act of 1906 which also pro

the retention of mineral rights by the tribe) received increasing sums in oil
lties. Thus began the wild spending that made newspaper headlines throughout
country — Osages bought expensive cars, built fine homes and invested in stock,
estate, furs, furniture and jewelry with their newly-acquired wealth.

regulations as they were during the 18th Century.

Just as the tribe changed economically in the 20th Century, it also changed demographically. Of the original 2229 Osage allotees, 860 were full-bloods and 1369 were mixed-bloods. By 1952 the population had increased to 5307, of which 9% were full-bloods and more than 65% less than one-fourth Indian blood. In 1970, the census enumerated 8244 Osages with 323 listed as full-bloods. Rather than concentrating on one reservation, members of the tribe have taken up residence in more than 300 different communities and in at least 36 states. The largest single group of those away from the state of Oklahoma live in southern California. Yet most of those Little Ones of more than one-half Indian blood continue to live in Oklahoma, the majority still in Osage County. Like its focus of population, the tribe's age distribution has also altered: by 1970 nearly 50% of the Osages were under 21 years of age. Thus not only is there a decided trend toward biologic assimilation with the white man, but the tribal population is growing more youthful.

The Osage national council has provided effective leadership for the Little Ones in recent decades. Organized according to the provisions of the amended allotment act, the council consists of a principal chief, an assistant chief, and eight councilmen. These officers are selected

CIPAL CHIEF FRED LOOKOUT, a great leader of the Osage Nation: he held office
n terms. He died in office on August 28, 1949.

quadrennially by an electorate composed of tribal members 21 years of age or over whose name appeared on the last quarterly annuity roll. As the Osages were specifically exempted from the provisions of the Wheeler-Howard Act and the Oklahoma Indian Welfare Act, the tribal council operates under neither a constitution nor a corporate charter. Instead it functions somewhat like a board of directors of a corporation, exercising authority in leasing the tribal estate, in determining the bonus value of any tract offered for lease, in the use of tribal funds, and in the administration of the tribal reserves located at Grey Horse, Hominy, and Pawhuska.

The council has used its authority well. Between 1935 and 1947 it funded a health clinic operated at the agency. Also, in 1947 it instituted litigation before the Indian Claims Commission in Washington and successfully won a judgment in 1955 amounting to $864,107. The tribe based its claim upon inequities associated with residence in and removal from Kansas.

The principal chiefs of the Osages have included many capable and distinguished leaders, one of whom is the present chief, Sylvester J. Tinker. One of the outstanding leaders of the past was Fred Lookout, who served continuously from 1924 to 1949.

In recent decades an increasing number of Osages have taken advantage of educational opportunities. In the early years of the century,

88

*Photograph by John Griffin*

PICTURE OF THE OSAGE INDIAN AGENCY shows the "Million Dollar Elm," so
because in the early days it was under this same Elm where the Oil Lease
ons were held. Could this Elm talk it would tell you about the greatest sale
etted the Osages over $14,000,000.00.

children of primary age attended either the government boarding school, the St. Louis Mission School, or the St. John's Mission School. For advanced education, they selected Bacone College, Haskell Institute, and Carlisle Indian School. After the government and parochial boarding schools closed (the government school in 1921, St. John's in 1915, and St. Louis in 1948), Osage parents have sent their youngsters either to Catholic day schools at Pawhuska and Fairfax or public schools. In 1925 the first full-blood Osage graduated from public high school, while in 1935 thirty-one more graduated and in 1952 ninety-eight more. In 1970, several hundred Osage young men and women were enrolled in different high schools throughout the area. Others have also availed themselves of opportunities for higher education, attending and graduating from institutions in Oklahoma and elsewhere.

This increasing interest in formal education suggests a growing measure of tribal integration into the total community life. Mixed-bloods are generally well integrated, though full-bloods have tended to retain their Indian identity. Residing in towns or on their ranches, the Little Ones have acquired beautiful homes and tasteful furnishings. Many have traveled extensively, and some have gained local, national and international reputations by their successes in the arts and the professions. Among the latter are numbered Chief Fred Lookout, an alumnus of Carlisle Indian School, and John Joseph Mathews, graduate of Oxford University and author of *Wah'Kon-tah* and the poetic-like *The Osages.* Other notables include Marjorie Tallchief, once leading ballerina with the Paris Opera, her sister, Marie Tallchief, lately the prima ballerina of the New York City Ballet, and Clarence L. Tinker, (see photo page 49) General of the U. S. Air Force in Hawaii on the occasion of his death at the Battle of Midway in 1942.

The service and death of Gen. Tinker suggests another aspect of Osage integration into the white community. The tribe totally supported the United States in its two World Wars during the 20th Century. On the occasion of the First World War, the council set aside a 5000 acre tract as a Naval Oil Reserve, while individuals purchased $2,500,000 worth of Liberty Bonds and contributed liberally to the Red Cross. One-third of the men eligible volunteered for military service. Likewise, during World War II, 519 members of the Osage tribe served in the armed forces, and of that number 26 were killed in action or while in training. Nine Osages were awarded decorations for meritorious service, 50 served as commissioned officers, and 47 acted as non-commissioned officers.

Once totally and irrevocably committed to *Wa-kon-da,* the Little Ones through the course of the last several decades have come to more

92

*Photograph by John Griffin*

MARY LOOKOUT STANDING BEAR

fully accept the white man's God. Consummating the historic mission efforts of the black robes, the Osages remain strongly Roman Catholic, although some Protestant sects have made converts — the Baptists, Methodists, and Friends have growing memberships within the tribe.

But it would be a mistake to conclude that the Little Ones have forsaken entirely their ancient heritage or completely and successfully integrated into the white community. Some still belong to the Native American Church, a fellowship that has declined in recent years. In 1918 it had approximately 25 congregations with individual memberships of 20 to 30 people. Osage members of the Catholic parishes at Pawhuska and Fairfax have demonstrated their reluctance to completely forget the past by forming their own altar societies. Still others have suffered identity crises that come with the adoption of alien ways and the pressures of unexpected wealth. Though their number is not large, these have turned to alcoholism and drug addiction. Finally, since the discovery of oil on the reservation, the majority of the tribe has relied upon the headright payment as their primary source of income instead of joining the mainstream of American economic life.

## THE FUTURE

The Osage people have had a history of excitement, a culture of substance, and a tradition of meaning. It is hard to imagine a future in which the Little Ones do not participate. Yet there will be some problems. For example, the trend toward biologic assimilation presents the prospect that the Osages may forget their past, their traditions and their identity. As a people cannot know where they are going or who they are if they do not know where they have been and who they were, the tribe will have to make a conscious effort to preserve whatever remains of the past. The effort should be made not so that Osage young men and women can separate themselves from the predominant white society but that they can better participate in it. Knowledge of oneself brings confidence, and confidence brings success.

Another problem that will confront the Little Ones is economic in character. Their land base is already eroded, and their oil and gas reserves are rapidly being depleted. To be sure, primary recovery of petroleum will continue and water-floor secondary recovery remain successful, but these have their limits. "The Osage" should produce for at least another 20 years and provide tribal revenues averaging more than $4 million per year. Yet as with all minerals, the oil and gas deposits will play out, and the tribe will have to look to other sources for economic survival.

Several alternatives to petroleum royalties exist. There are extensive deposits of limestone,

96

*Photograph by John Griffin*

E CHILDREN – Dana and Asa Cunningham and baby Deanna Rector – inherit
finity for the land and nature.

sand, sandstone and coal underlying the tribal reservation. All of these minerals with the exception of coal could be mined more intensively. The grade of coal, however, is such that the international market condition will retard immediate exploitation. Increased agricultural and ranching activities are also possible, but the development of the tourist trade has greater promise. The excellent museum at Pawhuska, the colorful tribal ceremonies, the recreational facilities, and the hospitality of the people could and should be parlayed into a profitable enterprise.

The economic transition that must come with the depletion of oil and gas reserves can be greatly facilitated by a more formally educated population. Educational grants by the Bureau of Indian Affairs and the tribal council will encourage Osage youngsters to acquire skills and an awareness that will ensure the future existence of the Little Ones.

With attention to tradition, economic development and education, the Osage people will meet the challenges of tomorrow. In so doing, they will further enrich the American heritage.

# THE SEAL OF THE OSAGE NATION

THE SEAL OF THE OSAGE NATION was adopted by the Osage Tribal Council on May 4, 1955. It has superimposed on a circular field of gold an arrowhead of blue centered with a buckskin and eagle feather fan crossed by a symbolic pipe of peace. The gold field is symbolic of tribal prosperity; the arrowhead, when used in the arrow, was an instrument of the hunt and of war; the pipe became a symbol of peace since it was smoked at the time of treaty-making to seal the pact between the Indian and the white man and to indicate peaceful and friendly relations between them; and the eagle feather fan is a symbol of authority or high office in clan or tribal affairs.

# SUGGESTED READING

Literature dealing with the entirety of the Osage story is not an extensive as one might think. In the main, the books listed below relate to different periods of tribal history and should be available in most major libraries. Shorter and more technical studies may be found in several scholarly journals.

COHEN, FELIX S. *Handbook of Federal Indian Law.* Washington: Government Printing Office, 1942.

An invaluable aid in unraveling the many laws that relate to the Osage as well as other tribes.

FOREMAN, GRANT. *Advancing the Frontier, 1830-1860.* Norman: University of Oklahoma Press, 1933.

Thorough study of relationships between enigrant and resident Indians; excellent on different councils.

*Indians and Pioneers: The Story of the American Southwest before 1830.* New Haven: Yale University Press, 1930.

Best account of the Osage-Cherokee conflict to 1830.

*Pioneer Days in the Early Southwest.* Cleveland: The Arthur H. Clark Company, 1926.

A solid study of Indian Territory during the 1830's.

101

*The Last Trek of the Indians.* Chicago: University of Chicago Press, 1946.

Chapter 15 deals with the Osages on their Kansas reservation.

GLASSCOCK, C. B. *Then Came Oil: The Story of the Last Frontier.* Indianapolis: The Bobbs-Merrill Company, 1938.

A well-written narrative that relates the heyday of oil on the Osage reservation.

GRAVES, WILLIAM W. *Early Jesuits at Osage Mission.* St. Paul, Kansas: W. W. Graves, c. 1916.

The only study of the Catholic mission effort in Kansas.

*The First Protestant Osage Missions, 1820-1837.* Oswego, Kansas: The Carpenter Press, 1949.

The first comprehensive account of Union and Harmony Missions.

HYDE, GEORGE E. *Indians of the Woodlands.* Norman: University Oklahoma Press, 1962.

Controversial and stimulating study of the pre-historic Osages.

LaFlesche, Francis. *The Osage Tribe: Rite of the Chiefs; Savings of the Ancient Men* in *The Thirty-sixth Annual Report of the Bureau of American Ethnology, 1914-1915.* Washington: Government Printing Office, 1921.

Splendid ethnological report recording some of the best of Osage materials.

McDermott, John Francis (ed). *Tixier's Travels on the Osage Prairies,* trans. by Albert J. Salvan. Norman: University of Oklahoma Press, 1940.

Very readable journal recording Osage lifeways in 1840.

Mathews, John Joseph. *The Osages: Children of the Middle Waters.* Norman: University of Oklahoma Press, 1962.

Lengthy but poetic account of the Little Ones to 1906.

*Wah'Kon-tah: The Osage and the White Man's Road.* Norman: University of Oklahoma Press, 1932.

Sensitive portrayal of Laban J. Miles' career as Osage agent after 1878.

Osage Agency. *The Osage People and Their Trust Property.* Anadarko: Bureau of Indian Affairs, 1953.

Excellent statistical study of the period since 1906.

## THE AUTHOR

W. DAVID BAIRD, who holds a Ph.D. degree from the University of Oklahoma, is an associate professor of History at the University of Arkansas. A native of Oklahoma, he has long been interested in the Indian tribes resident in that State. Baird is the author of *Peter Pitchlynn: Chief of the Choctaws* (University of Oklahoma Press, 1972). He has also written a number of articles in professional journals on the American Indian. Assisted by a grant from the American Philosophical Society, his present research interest is the history of the Quapaw Indians.